MOMMY COMES BACK

By Courtney Corson

I don't like when Mommy leaves.

Where is Mommy?

Mommy is going grocery shopping.

I am **sad**.

But I'm ok. I can color.

Where is Mommy?

Mommy is going to work.

I am **crying**.

But I'm ok. I can hug my stuffed animal.

Where is Mommy?
Mommy is going to the coffee shop.

I am **frustrated**.

But I'm ok. I can squeeze a pillow.

Where is Mommy?
Mommy is going to walk the dog.

I am **angry**.

But I'm ok. I can read a book.

Where is Mommy?

Mommy is going to the store.

I am **nervous**.

But I'm ok. I can take deep breaths.

Where is Mommy?// Mommy is going to mow the lawn.

I am **hesitant**.

But I'm ok. I can watch out the window.

Where is Mommy?
Mommy is going to the restaurant.

I am **curious**.

But I'm ok. I can pretend to cook.

Mommy always comes back.

I am happy!

I'm ok.

Copyright 2023 Courtney Corson

All Rights Reserved

Written by Courtney Corson 2023

Illustrated by Federica Calloni 2023

www.ingramcontent.com/pod-product-compliance
Lightning Source LLC
Chambersburg PA
CBRC100724060526
44119CB00085B/364